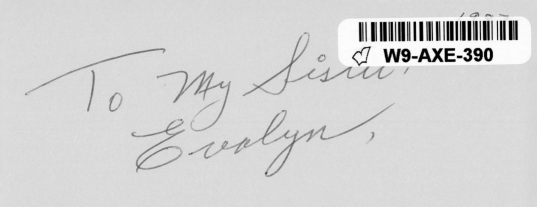

To My Sister,
Evelyn,

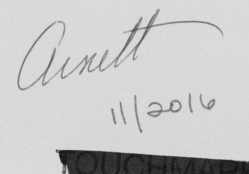

Arnett
11/2016

Thinking of You, My Sister

A collection of poems
Edited by Susan Polis Schutz

Blue Mountain Press T.M.

Boulder, Colorado

Library of Congress Catalog Card Number: 87-71583
ISBN: 0-88396-258-6

The following works have previously appeared in Blue Mountain Arts publications:

"To My Sister," by Davin Williams; and "It's so nice having you for my sister . . .," by Gwenda Isaac Jennings. Copyright © Blue Mountain Arts, Inc., 1984. "For My Sister," by Emma Kercek; "I'm Glad You Are My Sister," by Judith L. Sloan; "Sisters and Best Friends," by Gwenda Isaac Jennings; and "I'm Lucky to Have You as a Sister and a Friend," by Rosemary DePaolis. Copyright © Blue Mountain Arts, Inc., 1985. "Thinking of You, My Sister," "Sister, You're So Important to Me," and "A Family Is Love," by Collin McCarty. Copyright © Blue Mountain Arts, Inc., 1986. "Forever My Sister, Always My Friend," "Dear Sister," "Most of all, you're my sister . . .," and "Sister, It Means So Much to Have You in My Life," by Carey Martin; "You're Always Close in My Heart, Sister" and "You're One of the Nicest People I Know, Sister," by Lindsay Newman; "Though We're Apart Now, Sister . . ." and "Sister, You're Still My Closest Friend," by Adrian Rogers; "A Sister So Dear," by Collin McCarty; "I'll Always Be Glad You Are My Sister," by Deborah Butler DeVaney; and "To My Sister," by Deanna Beisser. Copyright © Blue Mountain Arts, Inc., 1987.

Thanks to the Blue Mountain Arts creative staff.

ACKNOWLEDGMENTS appear on page 62.

Manufactured in the United States of America
First Printing: October, 1987

Blue Mountain Press INC.

P.O. Box 4549, Boulder, Colorado 80306

CONTENTS

Forever My Sister, Always My Friend

We've always been friends . . .
and I know, more than anything,
that we always will be.

But you're also my sister,
        and because of that,
we share an understanding
        that goes beyond
what two friends can share.
There are things I can tell you
that I can't say to anyone else . . .
and I think that you feel the same way
        about me.
I am comforted by that thought, and
by the knowledge that —
        no matter what happens —

I'll always have you,
and you'll always have me,
to talk to, to confide in,
        and to walk with in every tomorrow.

That's real friendship.
        That's understanding and family love
        and security and faith.

        And that, to me . . . is great.

— Carey Martin

My Sister, Thank You

Thank you for all the moments
   we've shared —
moments filled with shared feelings
   and thoughts,
dreams and wishes, secrets,
   laughter and tears,
and above all, friendship.
Each precious second will be treasured
   in my heart forever.

Thank you for taking time —
time to stop and take an interest in me;
time to listen to my problems
   and help me find the solutions,
and most of all,
time to smile at me and show you care.

Thank you for being you —
　　you're a wonderful person.
You were there when I needed you,
　　to confide in and to ask advice from.
Through you, I began to understand
　　and even like myself.

How can I ever tell you how much I care
　　for you?
Thank you, my sister.

　　　　　　　　　　　　— Linda Scharnhorst

To My Sister

I just want you to know . . .
how important you are to me,
to know that you care
and understand me
to know that you trust
and believe in me.
I just want you to know . . .
how wonderful it is having you
as a sister,
to know that you are always
there for me
to know that you will always
be my friend.
I just want you to know . . .
that I know how wonderful you are,
that I do care
and that I do love you.

— Davin Williams

Sister, It Means So Much
to Have You in My Life

You know me like no other
person ever will.
You know the story of my life,
for it is written on many of
     the same pages as yours.
You know my faults and weaknesses,
     my insecurities and my doubts,
          and still. . .you like me
               anyway.

You're good to me.
And you're good for me.
You're the only person who
I know for certain would be there
trying to hold my spirits up,
if my whole world
     came crashing down.

I can't tell you
how much it means to have you
        in my life.
All I can say
        . . . is that I can't imagine
                being here without you.

        You're wonderful.
                You really are.

                        — Carey Martin

It's so nice having you
for my sister . . .

You're the best kind of sister —
the kind who listens when I need
    to talk;
who cares when there is no one else.
You've given me courage when I
    had none
and strength when I needed it.
You've given compassion and
    kindness at any time.

You've always been there —
ready to listen, understand and
love me for who I am.
You are my best friend . . .
and I love you.

— Gwenda Isaac Jennings

For My Sister

Together we shared a child's world.
We talked, we disagreed,
we shared personal hurts and joys,
and the older we grew,
the stronger the bond between us became.
I was always so proud to have you as
my sister.
Now life has taken us down separate paths,
but your well-being and happiness
will always be foremost in my thoughts.
Neither the span of miles nor years
between us can ever change the feelings
I have for you . . . I love you.

— Emma Kercek

Thinking of You,
My Sister

I hope that it brings you a smile
to know how much
   you've been on my mind.

Every time I think of you,
I wish we lived closer together . . .
but I know
   in my heart
that we will always be
as near and as dear to each other
   as sisters and best friends
                  can be.

— Collin McCarty

I'm Glad You Are My Sister

When I say to someone,
"She is my sister . . . ,"
it is impossible to keep the warmth
from my voice
or the love from my eyes.
I not only admire you,
but like you as well;
we share a bond even
     more unbreakable
than that of family . . .

To have lived through the pains
of growing up together
and still be able to say these words
is quite amazing.
Too many people cannot say them.
But we are closer now than ever,
and I want you to know
that I am very, very glad
you are my sister.

— Judith L. Sloan

I'm Lucky to Have You
as a Sister and a Friend

Sisters are like friends
You share
    problems and secrets,
       joys and sorrows
You have
    misunderstandings
    that seldom
       last long
But most of the time,
    you are in agreement

A sister, like a friend,
    is always there . . .
       ready to listen,
       willing to help,
       telling you
          just what you
          want to hear

She is full of
  love and care,
    warmth and understanding
And is a lot of fun
  to be with

A sister and a friend
  in one is rare
That is why
  I consider myself
    so lucky . . .
Because
  I have both
A sister and a friend
  in you.

— Rosemary DePaolis

A Family Is Love

Wherever we go,
   and whatever we do,
let us live with this
remembrance in our hearts . . .
   that we are family.

What we give to one another
comes full circle.
May we always be
   the best of friends;
may we always be one another's
   rainbow on a cloudy day;

as we have been yesterday
and today to each other,
    may we be so blessed
        in all our tomorrows . . .
        over and over again.

For we are a family,
    and that means love
            that has no end.

— Collin McCarty

My Sister, My Forever Friend

You have always been
my true friend.
The fact is not
that I will always
have you near me,
but that you will always
be near me . . .
in my heart.
Forever
is a binding word,
but I do care for you
in that way.
Above all else in life,
I find for myself
what's most true
through knowing you.

So no matter
what time brings,
always know that I love you.
I'm so glad
you're my sister . . .
I'm so thankful
you're my friend.

— Janice Lamb

To My Sister

It seems like only yesterday
that we were kids together,
and we had so much fun.
Now we live in different places.
And sometimes,
I find myself feeling a little
sentimental, happy, and sad
all at once.
I miss you and your smiles,
and I think about how very
special you are to me.
I know we are miles apart,
but that will never change the
feelings in my heart for you.

— Deanna Beisser

You're Always Close in My Heart, Sister

Though it seems that we seldom
spend time together,
you're still, and always will be,
an important part of my life.
And I just didn't want to let
another day go by
without telling you
that I miss you
and I care about you
very much.

— Lindsay Newman

I'm Here for You, My Sister

Sometimes when I look at you, Sister,
I see so much of myself —
I see you struggling to find yourself,
I see your independent spirit
searching to establish your own
    individual identity,
trying to follow your own beliefs,
dream your own dreams.
I know what you are going through,
    Sister,
and I know what a difficult time
    this is for you.

I want you to know that even though
   you'll make mistakes — as I have —
I will stand beside you,
I will defend your right to be you.
I believe in your goodness —
I feel confident that you are on your way
   to becoming a strong and wonderful
person.

I want you to know —
I am, and I always will be,
very proud that you are my sister.

                              — Karen Poynter Stevens

To My Sister

You have never failed me in
  my troubled times.
Even though I felt alone and unable
  to cope,
you provided enough light to help me
  see clearly,
to find the solutions that were right.
You have been faithful to the bonds
  that hold us.
Your loving way has been an inspiration
  to live life to the best of my
   ability.
Whatever I accomplish in this life,
  your hand is in it.
Whatever happiness I provide others,
  your smile assists in.
Whatever my contribution is,
  it is because of one you made to me.

You are forever a source of joy,
  and I wish to thank you
for being part of my life.

       — Linn Brosnan

Though We're Apart Now, Sister,
We Share a Lifetime Closeness

The time has flown, hasn't it?

I can't believe it's been so long!
Still . . . I feel as close to you as ever,
and I want you to know that I do.

I think it must be the case that,
coming from a close and caring family,
we always keep in our hearts
    the feelings,
        the memories,
            and the meaning of what
                it is to be related.
As part of a family, we have shared
experiences that no others have ever
shared in exactly the same way.

The places we have lived; the mother and
father we have been loved by; the lessons
learned and the laughter we have come by;
a thousand unique things have made us
and taken us to where we are today.

I'll never stop being proud
of being related to you.
And I'll always feel the closeness,
no matter how far the distance
or how distant the days.

— Adrian Rogers

A Sister So Dear

Thoughts of you
take special care of me
when I'm feeling
low or a little lost.

They find me
and take me back
to the times when you and I
were growing up together.
Thoughts of you
and what you mean to me
chase away shadows and
bring me sunlit memories of
how close we were, of secrets
we never shared with anyone else,

of borrowed clothes and shared lives,
of dreams that sometimes came true
and worries that almost never did.

There are times when I need you, my sister.
But I want you to know
    that when I do . . .
        you always come through.

— Collin McCarty

I have been blessed by your
love and support,
my sister and true friend . . .

Some of my closest friends
don't know my deepest secrets,
dreams, or lifetime goals.
Only the special people,
whom I can trust
and who I feel will accept
and understand me
despite my flaws,
are let into my heart.

Sharing myself
means taking a risk
in exposing too much,
a risk in being rejected.
But through our relationship,

you have showered me
with support and encouragement.

You listen to my dreams
when they seem out of reach
and give me the strength
to succeed.
I have been blessed by your love,
and that is why I share
all that I am with you,
my sister and my true friend.

— Katers Martin

Sister, the Bond We Share
Grows Stronger Every Day

When I think about us getting older,
I realize that every year
the bonds of love and understanding
that we share
keep growing stronger and deeper.
It is hard for me to be miles away

when I'd rather
see you face to face,
but you know that
wherever you are, whatever day it is,
I always send
my love to you.

— Deanna Beisser

Being Family, Being Friends

We shared the same house
   that we called home.
We shared the best of times
   and some troubled times, too.
Being a family was good;
   being friends is great.
People often take feelings for granted;
   words go unspoken,
      feelings unexpressed.
That is not good enough for me.
I want you to know how great my life is
   because you are a part of it.
Without my asking,
   you are always there for me.

I am proud of you;
   I look up to you.
I will always be here for you,
   and I love you so much.
We may have grown up,
   but in my heart,
      we never grew apart.

— Nancy Hazel Davis

My Love for My Sister
Is Forever in My Heart

There comes a time when a sister
goes on to lead her separate life —
following the path
that was set for her.

And sometimes time slips away
too fast
and important things
can be left unsaid . . .
like how very much
I love you,
and how that love
extends to the one
you've chosen to share
your life with.
And even though
our paths may not
cross often enough anymore,
remember the love
that is in my heart,
and know that I will
always carry it with me.

— P. F. Heller

I Hope We'll Always Be Close as Sisters and Also as Friends

The closeness we have shared
over the past years
has helped us both through
some very trying times,
and we have become so much more
than sisters;
we have become special friends.

We have learned so many new things
about each other,
and these discoveries have made
both of us realize just how much
richer our lives are now
because we are sisters.

— Christine Anne Keller

Dear Sister,

I meant to tell you,
 long before now,
what a wonderful sister you are . . .

But since I never really
got around to telling you
what a marvelous person you are,
what an inspiration you are to me,
and what a beautiful woman you are
    inside, and outside, too . . .

I'll say it now, because it's
    something I wish you knew.

— Carey Martin

You're One of the Nicest
People I Know, Sister

You're a pleasure to talk to,
a pleasure to be with,
and a pleasure just to know.
And I hope you'll believe me
when I tell you that
I feel very fortunate to have
someone as special as you
in my life.

— Lindsay Newman

We Live Far Apart, Sister, but We'll Remain the Best of Friends

Our lives have gone in different directions,
and we live so far apart now.
I really miss our serious discussions
and spur-of-the-moment acts.
I'm meeting new people
   and making new friends,
but it's so strange
not having you here with me.
I knew all along what a special person
   you were,
but now that I don't get to see you
   as often as I'd like,

I've come to appreciate our friendship
   even more.
No one could ever replace the closeness
   that we share.
We have a friendship that will survive
   any distance put between it,
whether it be in miles or years.
I know deep in my heart that we
will always remain the best of friends.

— Cheryl L. Gatch

I Wish We Could
Spend More Time Together, Sister

I've been so busy lately,
trying to keep up with
all the things in my world,
that it's been a while
since I last saw you.
It's sad how fast the hours
in each day come and go,
leaving little time
for ourselves and our friends,
but today I'm taking the time
to say "Hi," and
I'm thinking about you,
hoping it won't be too long
until we can spend some time
together.

— Deanna Beisser

Sister, You're Still My
Closest Friend

Memories are not easily forgotten.
Some of the best remembrances
   I will ever hold in my heart
      are the ones that have to do
  with growing up
         with you.

It's easy to get lost in thought,
    thinking about how much we've shared,
   and smiling to realize
        how close we've always been.

But sometimes it's so hard
to be apart from the person
that I will always think of
    as my dearest and closest friend.

                    — Adrian Rogers

Most of all,
you're my sister . . .

You are my closest companion;
you are my best friend;
you are the person I most want
   to share the news with when
   things go right; and the one
   I rely on when things go wrong.
You are so many good things
   and so many qualities I love.

But most of all, you're my sister.
   And you're something special to me
   that no one else can ever be.

— Carey Martin

Sisters and Best Friends

We've shared everything, you and I.
Even a room
  filled with laughter and tears
  and all our hopes and fears.
We've shared secrets meant
  for no one but us.

Most of all, we've shared happiness.
There are so many wonderful memories
  with many more to come
  as we grow older . . . together
   as sisters . . .
    and as best friends.

— Gwenda Isaac Jennings

Dear Sister —

Yesterday, we planned our goals
and wondered about the beauties
life had to offer

Today, we share the blessings
of family, the memories of childhood,
and our hopes for the future

Tomorrow, we still will be together
in our minds and in our hearts, for
we are as one and I love you.

— Edith Schaffer Lederberg

Sister, there is a bond between
us that goes beyond friendship . . .

There is a bond between us
    that nothing can change.
We are so different from each other,
but there is a closeness between us
    that goes beyond friendship.
I'm always filled with joy
when we're together.
We don't spend as much time
        with each other
            as I would like

because of the miles that separate us,
but the time we do have is extra-important
 because of that.
I think about you a lot,
and I have many happy memories
 of our growing up together.
I'm so glad you are my sister.

— Harriet Meola

For my sister

As we grow older
I learn to appreciate you
            more and more.
When we were just children,
we had our disagreements,
      which was only natural,
but even then I knew
that you were a very special friend.

Throughout the years
you have shown me affection
and have always been there
when I needed someone.

Together we have shared
        secrets, laughter
and the joys of growing up.
And in that time
I hope that I have returned to you
some of the love
you have unselfishly given to me.
I am forever grateful
to have a sister like you.

— E. Lori Milton

I'll Always Be Glad
You Are My Sister

If I could choose the person
who would be my sister,
she would have a gentle spirit
and a strong will.
She would be kind,
courageous,
and never compromise her goals.
She would be someone I would
always be glad to have in my life.
She would be you.

— Deborah Butler DeVaney

Sister, You're So
Important to Me

Why is it that we
never seem to be able
to tell each other
how important we are
            to each other?

We can talk and joke about
so many things; we reminisce
about the times of our lives
when we were growing up;
we try to keep in touch
with each other's comings and goings . . .

But of all the things
I've ever said to you,
   I don't think I've ever said
      something that I feel inside
         and something I've always
           known was true . . .

And it is true; you're a very
   special part of my family
and a very important part of my life . . .
   and I love you.

               — Collin McCarty

ACKNOWLEDGMENTS

We gratefully acknowledge the permission granted by the following authors to reprint their works.

Linda Scharnhorst for "My Sister, Thank You." Copyright © Linda Scharnhorst, 1987. All rights reserved. Reprinted by permission.

Karen Poynter Stevens for "I'm Here for You, My Sister." Copyright © Karen Poynter Stevens, 1987. All rights reserved. Reprinted by permission.

Linn Brosnan for "To My Sister." Copyright © Linn Brosnan, 1987. All rights reserved. Reprinted by permission.

Katers Martin for "I have been blessed by your love . . ." Copyright © Katers Martin, 1987. All rights reserved. Reprinted by permission.

Deanna Beisser for "Sister, the Bond We Share Grows Stronger Every Day" and "I Wish We Could Spend More Time Together, Sister." Copyright © Deanna Beisser, 1987. All rights reserved. Reprinted by permission.

Janice Lamb for "My Sister, My Forever Friend." Copyright © Janice Lamb, 1982. All rights reserved. Reprinted by permission.

Nancy Hazel Davis for "Being Family, Being Friends." Copyright © Nancy Hazel Davis, 1987. All rights reserved. Reprinted by permission.

P. F. Heller for "My Love for My Sister Is Forever in My Heart." Copyright © P. F. Heller, 1987. All rights reserved. Reprinted by permission.

Christine Anne Keller for "I Hope We'll Always Be Close as Sisters and Also as Friends." Copyright © Christine Anne Keller, 1987. All rights reserved. Reprinted by permission.

Cheryl L. Gatch for "We Live Far Apart, Sister . . ." Copyright © Cheryl L. Gatch, 1987. All rights reserved. Reprinted by permission.

E. Lori Milton for "For my sister." Copyright © E. Lori Milton, 1982. All rights reserved. Reprinted by permission.

Edith Schaffer Lederberg for "Dear Sister." Copyright © Edith Schaffer Lederberg, 1984. All rights reserved. Reprinted by permission.

Harriet Meola for "Sister, there is a bond between us . . ." Copyright © Harriet Meola, 1987. All rights reserved. Reprinted by permission.

A careful effort has been made to trace the ownership of poems used in this anthology in order to obtain permission to reprint copyrighted materials and to give proper credit to the copyright owners.

If any error or omission has occurred, it is completely inadvertent, and we would like to make corrections in future editions provided that written notice is made to the publisher: BLUE MOUNTAIN PRESS, INC., P.O. Box 4549, Boulder, Colorado 80306.

Thinking of You, My Sister